Small World

The CAFOD'

Sheila Cassidy * Celia Deane-Drummond
Joseph Donders * John Rawsthorne
Wendy M. Wright * Phumzile Zondi

Small World

Reflections on the Scripture Readings for Lent 2004

CAFOD
just one world

DARTON·LONGMAN+TODD

First published in Great Britain in 2003 by

CAFOD
Romero Close
Stockwell Road
London SW9 9TY

Darton, Longman and Todd Ltd
1 Spencer Court
140–142 Wandsworth High Street
London SW18 4JJ

ISBN 0 232 52522 6

Note: the Hebrew numbering of the Psalms is used. From Psalm 10 to 147 this is ahead of the Greek and Vulgate numbering which is used in some psalters.

Cover photo: Martin Leuders
Cover design: Garry Lambert

Text designed and produced by Sandie Boccacci
Set in 9.5/13pt Palatino
Printed and bound in Great Britain
by Cox & Wyman, Reading

Contents

About the authors		vii
Introduction	Brendan Walsh	ix
Ash Wednesday to Saturday after Ash Wednesday	Sheila Cassidy	2
First week of Lent	Sheila Cassidy	10
Second week of Lent	Celia Deane-Drummond	24
Third week of Lent	John Rawsthorne	38
Fourth week of Lent	Phumzile Zondi	52
Fifth week of Lent	Joseph Donders	66
Holy Week	Wendy M. Wright	80
About CAFOD		99

About the authors

Sheila Cassidy is a writer, lecturer, counsellor and broadcaster. In 1975 she was tortured in Chile for treating a revolutionary - an episode she recounts in her autobiographical work, *Audacity to Believe*. She is also the author of *Good Friday People* and *Sharing the Darkness* (all published by DLT).

Celia Deane-Drummond is Professor of Theology and the Biological Sciences at Chester College of Higher Education. She lectures worldwide and is the director of the Centre for Religion and the Biosciences. Her many books include *A Handbook on Theology and Ecology* and *Creation Through Wisdom: Theology and the New Biology*.

Joseph Donders, a priest of the Society of the Missionaries of Africa (the 'White Fathers'), is currently Director of Mission and Cross-Cultural Studies at Washington Theological Union. He has worked as a missionary, teacher, lecturer and chaplain in Kenya, Uganda, India, the Netherlands and North America. He is the author of several books including: *The Fullness of Time* (published by CAFOD).

John Rawsthorne is the Bishop of Hallam, and the Chairman of CAFOD.

Wendy M. Wright teaches on the Theology faculty at Creighton University (Omaha, Nebraska). She is the author of several academic studies on the Salesian spiritual tradition and several works of popular spirituality and prayer, including *Sacred Heart* and *The Vigil: Keeping Watch in the Season of Advent* (both published by DLT).

Phumzile Zondi is an elder in the Uniting Presbyterian Church of Southern Africa and Coordinator of the Women and Gender Programme at the Institute for the Study of the Bible, a project of the School of Theology, University of Natal, Pietermaritzburg, South Africa.

Introduction

'It is all upside down.'

In Wendy Wright's reflection on the scripture readings for Passion Sunday she describes the way that Jesus so often spoke and acted in ways that shocked and confounded his first followers. They expected his entry into Jerusalem to be a moment of vindication, of triumph. Instead, he arrives on a donkey. They expected him to see off the soldiers who had come to arrest him. Instead, he allows himself to be dragged away in disgrace.

'It is all upside down.'

In our world, it is the winners, the powerful, who are the heroes. The 'leading' nations, the 'superpowers', are those who have the greatest military strength, those with the greatest capacity to use force to stay in control of events. We live as though the most precious and important thing in the world is power - won through violence, or the threat of violence. To follow Jesus means to unlearn every instinct, every knowing that we have lived with so far. It is not about power. It is not about winning. When the soldiers come, we are told to put down our swords. It is about living into the kingdom that, with his life and his death, he proclaimed.

The greatest amongst us are not the powerful who are served but those who serve.

'It is all upside down.'

We begin the journey of Lent each year determined to do our little bit to make this new kingdom a reality in our lives and in the world around us. We try to learn more about the problems of others, to accept and forgive those we live with and work with, to become more generous in our giving.

But as we pray, as we put ourselves humbly before God, something happens, the journey of Lent changes, the path we thought was before us muddies over and a new and different one opens up. When we reflect on the journey of Jesus we see his willingness to let others occupy the busy centre of the story, exercising their power, keeping a tight grip on events. He is willing to let go, not only or most interestingly material possessions, but also his reputation, his status in the eyes of others. He is humiliated. He willingly allows himself to be handed over to be crucified on the cross.

We become aware that Lent is not a time to elbow our way up to the moral high ground, but of learning to risk everything, to trust to the help of others and the grace of God, to speak the truth whatever it means for our position in the world, to relish the joy of receiving as well as of giving.

Those who have had the experience of working beside CAFOD's partners throughout the world particularly treasure the words of the Salvadorean theologian, Jon Sobrino, who explains that when we from the rich churches share funds with the churches that serve the poor, what takes place is far deeper than charity or even solidarity. What we receive is of a different and higher order than what we give. We receive a new inspiration in faith, a new understanding of ourselves.

We might have begun the journey of Lent thinking of ourselves as the ones who show compassion, the ones with hearts of gold. In reality, we learn to understand our own need for acceptance and forgiveness. We are not the ones who give. We are the ones who receive.

Brendan Walsh

Small World

The CAFOD/DLT Lent Book 2004

Sheila Cassidy

Ash Wednesday to Saturday after Ash Wednesday

Ash Wednesday

The desert experience

Jl 2:12–18; Ps 51; Co 5:20—6:2; Mt 6:1–6, 16–18

> *'For he is gracious and compassionate, slow to anger, rich in faithful love.'*
>
> (Joel 2:13)

I am completely useless at keeping Lent in the time-honoured way. On one Ash Wednesday I solemnly gave up sherry at breakfast time (not that I drink sherry for breakfast, you understand) and gave in to the desperate urge for a drink at ten past six that evening. Part of my problem is that as a tireless fighter in the battle of the bulge I have long since whittled down my culinary excesses to the bare minimum required to keep body and soul together, and any further cutbacks would lead to more neuroses than it's worth. (Even as I write this, I know it's not really true, but that's my excuse and I'm sticking to it.)

We think of Lent as a time when we try to find extra space for prayer and think of things to go without. But my personal theory is that Lent is a time for cutbacks and reflection chosen more by God than by us. By this I mean that just when life is going most smoothly, the fog may descend, leaving us weeping and floundering in our own tailor-made Lent. My own personal desert experience was a spell in solitary confinement in a Chilean gaol in the 1970s. Everything was laid on free of charge: pain, fear, bread and water. It was an enormously powerful experience, during which I felt very close to God.

We each have our 'private Lents': those times when lovers leave or beat us to a pulp; when parents die; when our kids take up drugs; or when we find ourselves suffering from cancer or some other hideous ailment. But what about the Lent that Christians share together, the liturgical season which is upon us? We could 'choose' our Lent, by giving up chocolate or wine as usual. Or we might instead carve out our own bit of desert time each day, not to 'do' anything but simply to listen to the God who calls us so urgently. I suspect that it's only through this kind of 'waste-of-time' prayer that we will come to know in our dry, dry bones, the truth of Joel's words: that the Lord is all tenderness and compassion, slow to anger and rich in graciousness.

Thought for the day

The Lord calls me by name
to waste time with him as lovers do
gazing at the sea or into the flame of a candle.

Prayer

Lord of the Desert,
give me the strength to make time for you this Lent.
Teach me to listen for your voice in the rustle of leaves in the wind
and in the silence of my own heart.
Amen.

Choose life

Dt 30:15–20; Ps 1; Lk 9:22–25

> *'This day I set before you life or death, blessing or curse. Choose life then . . .'*
>
> (Deuteronomy 15:19)

Life seems such an obvious choice, doesn't it, and yet so many choose death or the way that leads to it. I am thinking at this moment of one of my clients, David, a young man from a 'good' family who has a problem with addiction to drugs and alcohol. Just when I thought he had been making progress, planning to go to university in the Autumn, he failed to turn up for an appointment. I haven't heard from him since.

The last I heard, David was in London, and my guess is that he's probably using drugs again. I tried so hard to encourage him when he was down, to strengthen his fragile self-esteem and to help him summon up some discipline: but I failed. Perhaps I'm not a good enough therapist, or perhaps David has deliberately chosen death because he can't face life, and I must learn to live with my sense of impotence and heartache.

Where is God in David's desert of heroin and needles, in that dark and lonely cavern of despair? This much I know: God is right there alongside him, injecting, vomiting, weeping in shame and self-disgust. For our God is a suffering God, who has pitched his tent in the slums with the *anawim*, the broken ones of our modern world. This is a hard piece of theology to swallow. It's so much easier to think of God transcendent: out there, somewhere, in Glory, than it is to accept the revelation of God imminent, with a human face and bloodshot eyes.

Perhaps this Lent is a time to get to know God disguised in the outcast, the refugee or the terrorist caged in Guantanamo Bay. Think about it over a coffee and a chocolate biscuit and remember the passage in Matthew 25: 'I was hungry . . .'

Thought for the day

God came to save sinners, not the just.

Prayer

Lord, I pray for addicts and drunkards
and all the broken, unacceptable people you love so much.
Show me what I can do to help when I find you lying by the roadside.
Amen.

Dealing with the avalanche

Is 58:1–9; Ps 51; Mt 9:14–15

> *'Is not this the sort of fast that pleases me: to break unjust fetters, to undo the thongs of the yoke, and to let the oppressed go free.'*
>
> (Isaiah 58:6)

Here we have Isaiah eloquently campaigning on behalf of Amnesty International, Christian Aid, CAFOD and all the other aid organizations. We know what God thinks of those who are meticulous in their religious observance but who ignore people in need. But what are we to do with the avalanche of ever more sophisticated requests for our charity on behalf of the hungry, the imprisoned and the exile? Before I retired I had a long list of small standing orders made payable to those charities which appealed to me or which had caught me on a vulnerable day. Then, when I gave up work and my income plummeted I panicked and cancelled all but two: Oxfam and the Medical Foundation for the Care of Victims of Torture. For the past year I have been ruthlessly binning appeals on behalf of the deaf, the blind, the hungry and the mentally ill: I can't cope with it all and I expect you can't either. I especially hate the ones that enclose a cheap biro or a shiny new 20p piece. I bin the biro and put the coin in my piggy bank (which the cleaning lady raids when I forget to leave any money out for her).

I've never found the right answer to the difficult

question of the good stewardship of my hard-earned wealth. When I came out of the convent I vowed never to buy anything new for my flat and to do without a vacuum cleaner, washing machine and television. It wasn't long, however, before my clothes were grey and the dust made my asthma bad and I was forced to behave like everyone else. I held out a little longer with the telly but then they broadcast *Brideshead Revisited* and I was done for.

Each of us has to work out for ourselves what we can afford to give and then get on with giving it with a smile, for as it says in the Bible, God loves a cheerful giver. Perhaps Lent is a suitable time to review our charitable giving. This year I think I'm going to support Medicin Sans Frontieres because I wish that I had done that kind of doctoring when I was young enough. What about you? Perhaps you should review your bank statements this morning while having your coffee and biscuits.

Thought for the day

The rain it raineth equally on the just and the unjust – but it rains especially hard on the homeless.

Prayer

Lord Jesus, teach me to be generous:
to give and not to count the cost,
to pass by on the other side of the street when approaching my favourite shop
to smile sweetly and give a pound to the man selling *The Big Issue,*
and another one to the woman collecting for Cancer Relief.
Amen

Each of us is called

Is 58:9–14; Ps 86:1–6; Lk 5:27–32

> *'Yahweh will always guide you ... he will give strength to your bones and you will be like a watered garden.'*
>
> (Isaiah 58:11)

'Your life shall be like a watered garden' is a powerful image in the Holy Land, where the sun shines bright and the earth is dry as a bone. The watered garden is the symbol of fecundity, of a life made fruitful for the sake of others. I have a particular interest at the moment in the phenomenon of call, or, as it is sometimes called, 'vocation'. I am filled with wonder at the flowering of so many lives.

My favourite, I think, is the story of Gladys Aylward, the London parlour maid who had the crazy idea that God was calling her to be a missionary in China. She saved up her wages and travelled by the Trans-Siberian Railway to Harbin, crossed to Japan and then back to Shanghai and thence into central China. There she worked, initially with another woman and then on her own, telling of the love of God to anyone who would listen. When war came she led a troop of over a hundred children through the Chinese countryside to a town where they would be cared for in safety. God did indeed give strength to her bones as she marched with the children and finally led her triumphant over the heights of the land.

When I was a convent school girl in the 1950s there was much talk of vocation. I remember a poster which had a finger pointing at the observer and the caption: 'Is God calling you to the Religious Life?' I suffered from frequent bouts of 'the divine measles' when I was a child, and became convinced that the only way to love God with all my heart and strength was to be a nun. I even 'tried my vocation' in my forties but eventually I asked to leave because I was so miserable.

These days, I see call differently. I believe that each one of us, you and me, is called by name, into the unknown, for a particular mission. For most of us, the call is not as extraordinary as that of a Gladys Aylward, but the Lord's promise is the same for each of is: if we do our level best to be a good mother or father, police officer or teacher, then will our light rise in the darkness and our shadow become like noon.

Thought for the day

God calls me by name, into the unknown, for a particular mission and he will give strength to my bones.

Prayer

Open my ears O God to hear your voice calling
and give me the courage to say Yes!

Sheila Cassidy

First week of Lent

First Sunday of Lent

The shelter of his wings

Dt 26:4–10; Ps 91; Ro 10:8–13; Lk 4:1–13

'My refuge, my fortress, my God in whom I trust.'
(Psalm 90)

This Sunday's readings are rich in both content and poetry. Psalm 90 takes me back to my monastic days and the sweetness of plain chant at the end of the day. How good it is to feel the shelter of his wings as we prepare for sleep, confident that we are God's beloved and safe from all danger. The trouble is, like a lot of Scripture, it doesn't seem to be entirely true: the beloved of God are murdered in their beds, they are raped, and betrayed. They fall off mountains, they are suffocated by molten lava and drown in tidal waves. So: how are we to take this sort of teaching? Desperately ill, and writing at a time of great turbulence, the English mystic Julian of Norwich was nevertheless convinced that 'all shall be well, and all manner of things shall be well'. All life, all safety, is a gift, not our right as Christians. But we cling to our stubborn hope that, in some way beyond our understanding, 'all shall be well.'

The most fruitful passage for me, however, is the passage from Deuteronomy in which Moses tells the people to reflect upon what we call their 'salvation history': the hand of God in their lives. This is a favourite task set by Jesuit retreat masters (and mistresses) and is often a useful exercise because it can fill us with a sense of wonder and gratitude. I remember how much I loved the nuns at school, and wondered what made them tick. I found that it was, of course, God. I remember too the different priests who have supported me over the years: especially Michael Hollings, who was chaplain at Oxford when I was an undergraduate. When I look back at the sand of my past life I see their footprints beside mine. And when there are no accompanying footprints I know that I was not alone: it was God who was carrying me and the single prints are not mine but his.

Thought for the day

Remember how the Lord carried you in the wilderness, as a father carries his child.

Prayer

Father God
be with us as we walk an unknown way.
Chide us, encourage us, support us,
and when the going gets really rough,
hoist us up on to your shoulders and carry us for a while.
Amen.

A light in the darkness

Lv 19:1–2, 11–18; Ps 19; Mt 25:31–46

'Your words are spirit, Lord and they are life'.
(Psalm 18)

The words of today's psalm say it all, don't they?

The word of God is alive and active, teaching, comforting, a light in the darkness and better than a known way. In my forties I spent eighteen months living under the shadow of a famous Benedictine monastery and then a further year and a half in a monastic convent for women. My monastic vocation, as I have said, came to naught but the daily exposure to the scriptures was worth all the heartache. In the Christian monastic life, men and women gather five times a day to recite the psalms and listen to the Scriptures being read. It was this which enticed me into the convent: God knows there was nothing else which appealed to me.

There is a process in the monastic way of life which I can only describe as becoming 'pickled', saturated, in the psalms. As you recite the psalter day after day, week after week, year after year, they take on an amazing familiarity. The best times for me were Lent and Advent, not just because the hymns were magical but because of the richness of the prophetic readings, especially Isaiah. Isaiah is my favourite writer in all the scriptures because he makes my timbers shiver with awe and delight. How anyone can read Isaiah and doubt that God loves them is a mystery to me. Listen to this:

'For the mountains may depart,
the hills be shaken,
but my love for you will never leave you.'

(Isaiah 54:10)

These are the words which for me are spirit and life, reviving the soul and giving light to the eyes. When I am Queen there will be large urban monasteries in every city centre and the workers will be able to come to midday prayer and vespers before they go home to cook supper. O brave new world!

Thought for the day

The law of the Lord is perfect, heed it now.

Prayer

Pickle us O God in your holy word
so that loving kindness becomes second nature to us.
Amen.

Goodbye, Charlie

Is 55:10–11; Ps 34; Mt 6:7–15

> *'The Lord is close to the broken hearted. He helps those whose spirit is crushed.'*
>
> (Psalm 34:18)

This morning, at ten thirty in the morning, my friend Charlie died of cancer at fifty-two years of age: a cruel fate for a lovely, generous-hearted man. Charlie was at the centre of the dog-walking fraternity on Plymouth Hoe. I would meet him once or twice a day as he and his little Westie, Dusty, walked with our friends Frank and Andy and Kenny and their motley collection of dogs, Sadie the Doberman, Bengie the Shitzu, Beattie the mongrel and Barney the Papillon. Each evening they would sit and watch the sun go down, drinking tea from a thermos while the dogs sat at their feet playing or eating the biscuits which Frank always carries in his pocket.

Community life is a funny thing: I hated it in the convent, and even the hospice which served Charlie so well in his last days felt claustrophobic. Among these gentle men, however, I have felt at home and found a different kind of comradeship. 'Teach us delight in simple things,' says the poem, 'and mirth that hath no bitter springs'. That's how it was with Charlie: delight in the antics of my Chow puppy Anka and sympathy for Mollie who was lamed by an overly boisterous Alsation. This is the bread and butter of human life: comradeship, hospitality and gentle humour with no back-biting, arrogance or pomposity.

How complicated we sometimes make our religion. While we argue about gay bishops or women priests or the number of angels dancing on the head of a pin, men like Charlie are being Christ, walking their dogs with lonely friends on the road to Emmaus. The older I get, the less I care about the intricacies of theology. What matters most to me now is people, that they should be fed and cared for, educated and liberated so that they may instinctively fulfil Jesus' amazing 'new' commandment:

> Love one another, as I have loved you: by this shall all men know that you are my disciples.

Goodbye, Charlie, and thanks for all you've taught me.

Thought for the day

The Lord is close to the broken hearted.
Instead of avoiding them, let us seek to comfort.

Prayer

We pray O Lord for those who mourn.
Give us words to comfort and the strength to share their pain.
Amen

What should we do?

Jon 3:1–10; Ps 51; Lk 11:29–32

> *'Jonah proclaimed, "Only forty days more and Ninevah will be overthrown." '*
>
> (Jonah 3:4)

I wonder how Jonah would get on today in London or New York? 'Repent!' he'd say, 'for the suicide bombers are coming, there will be nerve gas on the underground and the SARS virus in all your hospitals. Westminster Abbey will be blown up and the Royal Family taken hostage. Repent!' he'd say again, 'for God's sake, repent.'

And what would we do? We'd ask him what his intelligence was, we'd demand documentary evidence to back up his threats, and if he couldn't provide it, we'd laugh at him and dismiss him as a madman.

All this seems very far-fetched, although my guess is we're laughing a lot less now than we would have ten years ago. And yet, in a very real sense, we are hearing a warning like Jonah's now. The attack on the twin towers was described as a wake-up call to the decadent and selfish West, reminding us of how the fate of the peoples of the world is inter-connected, and spurring us to more just and generous behaviour towards the poorer nations and the oppressed of the world.

But the call remains unheeded. How hard it is to change patterns of structural injustice which are as familiar as our own skin. We are like ostriches, our heads firmly buried in the sand and our backs optimally exposed to attack. We take for granted the coffee on our shelves, the fresh fruit from California and the cut-price chickens in the supermarket without thinking for one minute about the wages or working conditions of those who produce and harvest them.

'So, what should we do?' you ask, irritated and unnerved. I'm as deeply enmeshed in the consumer culture as anyone. Like you, it feels as if all my energies are exhausted by my work. I teach, caring for the dying and listen to the confused and the broken hearted. Perhaps the answer is that we can only change one life: our own. This Lent, let us learn something about injustice, do something to support those who work for fair trade, teach our kids about the evils of poverty and racism, and recycle our rubbish. It's not a lot, but it's a beginning.

Thought for the day

Extract your head from the sand and look long and hard at the condition of your brothers and sisters.

Prayer

Lord, we are trapped like flies in amber
in our designer world of greed and consumerism.
Teach us to live simply –
that others may simply live.

Unfathomable God

Est 4:1–3, 5:12–14; Ps 138; Mt 7:7–12

> *'I thank you Yahweh, with all my heart, for you have listened to the cry I have uttered.'*
>
> (Psalm 138:1)

In today's Scripture readings we are face to face with one of the most awkward stumbling blocks for the faithful: what are we to believe when God does not answer our prayers?

I have a problem with prayers of intercession – surely God already has everything in hand? Yet I pray each evening as I drive towards home that that there will be a parking space and, surprise, surprise, there nearly always is. Is this coincidence or is God really answering my prayer? If he is, then it must be a seriously complicated operation. Let's see how it works: I'm approaching home as fast as the law allows and I send up a text message: 'Plse Ld, lt there b a pking spce.' God gets the message, jumps to and sends another message to my neighbour David that it's time to visit his partner, so David packs his bag, gets into his car and drives off to his friend's place on the other side of the river, just as I turn into the street.

This is clearly nonsense, but then surely asking for a parking space is a frivolous request which no one could expect God to take seriously. Surely God is busy about other things, sorting out anguished requests to find abducted children, cure dying mothers and keep the lid on restive volcanoes. The trouble is, only a certain proportion of these deeply serious requests are answered in the way we want, leaving the askers with broken hearts and broken faith.

How naïve we are! Do we believe that Almighty God, who created the universe, interferes with the workings of the world at our behest, arranging the sun to come out for our daughter's wedding day and then for the rain to fall for the crops the moment the guests have gone home? Actually, I do believe it – though I don't think it happens very often. I believe both that God has his world in hand and that he hears every one of our prayers, though why we so often do not get the answer to some of our most desperate requests I truly don't know. Like you, I can only struggle to live with the mystery – though one thing I am sure of: our God loves all his people, and listens to all of their cries for help with the same attentive hear: not just those who are 'good', not just those who go to church.

Thought for the day

You might as well stop struggling – the ways of the Lord are beyond our meagre powers of understanding.

Prayer

Holy, mysterious, unfathomable God,
we know that you hear our prayer
and that you love us,
despite all evidence to the contrary.
Amen

The wideness of God's mercy

Ez 18:21–28; Ps 130; Mt 5:20–26

> *'Would I take pleasure in the death of the wicked and not prefer to see him renounce his wickedness and live?'*
>
> (Ezekiel 18:23)

Many years ago I was attending Mass in a tiny Poor Clare convent on the Gulf Coast of Florida and worrying about a priest friend with AIDS. My worries were less about the state of his body than of his soul. Just as I was reflecting upon how God would feel about the betrayal of the vows my friend had made, the congregation of half a dozen nuns and a few lay people lumbered to its feet and began to sing a hymn which I had never heard before:

> There's a wideness in God's mercy
> like the wideness of the sea;
> there's a kindness in his justice
> which is more than liberty.
> For the love of God is broader
> than the measure of our mind
> and the heart of the Eternal
> is most wonderfully kind.
>
> (F W Faber 1814–63)

If ever there was a message for me straight from heaven that was it. 'Judge not, my good woman, lest you yourself be judged.' There's one more verse worth quoting:

But we make his love too narrow
by false limits of our own;
and we magnify his strictness
with a zeal he will not own.

The message is clear: the limits we put to God's love are our own, not God's. Ezekiel spells it out: if the wicked man renounces all the sins he has committed, he will live, not die. 'Yes', we say, 'that's all well and good, but it surely does not include paedophiles, child murderers and young thugs who beat up old ladies.' I'm afraid it does – we are all in the same boat, we are all sinners and what matters, for every one of us, is whether or not we repent, whether or not we turn to God and ask for his mercy and forgiveness.

The trouble is, a part of us does not want people to turn around their lives. We prefer things nice and simple, good people and bad people, us and them. Why do we not believe that a murderer might, with expert psychological and pastoral help, truly repent and become a good, compassionate, honourable person? Is it because we are unwilling to admit that he or she is damaged, a mixture of good and bad, and human - just like us? We find it hard to say, 'There, but for the grace of God, go I.'

Thought for the day

Does God find it easier to heal the dying or find a parking space than he does to turn around a man or woman's life?

Prayer

Give us a wide and gentle mercy O God.
Amen.

Love your enemy

Dt 26:16-19; Ps 119; Mt 5:43-48

> *'You must be perfect, just as your heavenly father is perfect.'*
>
> (Matthew 5:48)

'Be perfect . . . ' demands Jesus in today's gospel. Bit of a tall order, I reckon. Is it worth even trying? Let's look at the business of loving our enemies, for example: of all the unreasonable demands, surely that takes the biscuit. Am I expected to love my torturers? Is the mother of the murdered toddler expected to love the boys who killed him? Surely that is asking too much of grieving people. And yet, when the first agony of grief has passed, we must choose between hatred and forgiveness. And while hatred leads to loneliness and self-pity, forgiveness is the path to healing.

Forgiveness, I believe, is in the gift of God. It is not something we can achieve on our own. But there is hard thinking to do, too, in order to forgive. This involves trying to understand just why the other has wronged us. In my work with cancer patients and their families, there is one key quality required. This is the skill of empathy, which Carl Rogers described as 'the ability to enter the other's world as if it were your own, without losing the as-if quality'. In order to help them to develop empathy, I ask my trainees to 'create' an imaginary family. For example: Jane aged 30, a hairdresser, her husband Bill, a builder, and their three children, Mike, Sally and Jamie.

We then visit one of them with cancer. The purpose of this is to work out the emotions experienced by the patient and other members of the family, in the hope that the trainees will learn what to do in real life.

Perhaps the same technique might work in trying to understand those who wrong us. Let's take Jimmy, aged 20. His Mum, Mary, lives in a tower block with his three younger brothers and his alcoholic father, Dave, who regularly beats up Jimmy's Mum and the kids. Jimmy is out of work, bored and miserable, and dependent upon heroin. Without it, he feels lousy, and he steals to feed his habit because the blissful moment after shooting up is the only happiness which comes his way. Jimmy is a thief and a druggie, but perhaps by developing our skill of empathy, by trying to 'enter his world', we can begin to understand why he nicked our car radio, and begin on the path to forgiveness.

Thought for the day

Try not to criticise your neighbour until you've walked a mile in his moccasins.

Prayer

Lord, give us the strength and humility
to forgive those who have wronged us,
and the desire to understand why they did it.
Amen.

Celia Deane-Drummond

Second Week of Lent

Second Sunday of Lent

The way faith grows

Gen 15:5–12, 17–18; Ps 27; Ph 3:17—4.1; Lk 9:28–36

> *'Taking Abram outside the Lord said, "Look up to heaven and count the stars if you can. Such will be your descendents". Abram put his faith in the Lord, who counted this as making him justified.'*
>
> (Genesis 15:5)

Amidst the pressures of everyday life, the daily bombardment with news of natural catastrophes and devastations inflicted through war or human ignorance, it is hard to find time just to be with God and reflect on God's love and presence. Yet this is the invitation Abram as a very old man received: to remind himself of the Creator through witnessing the wonder of the created skies, and then to take the step of belief in God's promise. While his faith was as a gift, it came too from an active step on his part, a free decision to put his faith in the Lord, to take the risk against all the odds.

Why did Abram take this risk? He was prepared to trust, because he knew already something of the character of God. It was this step of faith that made him right with God, or 'justified'. He made his faith more concrete through acting out a liturgy. We may remember the story goes on to speak of how he could not quite believe that his elderly wife Sarah would be the means through which God's promise would come true. Eventually, slowly, it dawned on him, as it must on us, that God is not bound by our own expectations. We are called to act out what we dimly hear in God's Word, the call to take small steps to bring about the reign of God.

The disciples, too, needed to learn the same lesson. And, like them, we have to learn to tune in to hearing what God is saying, rather than simply interpreting events from our own perspective. Jesus was given a blessing on the mountain in preparation for his suffering to follow, yet perhaps even he could not have known the full extent of what obedience might mean. Today we have Jesus as an example of how to act and be in the world. We are told quite simply to 'Listen to him'. It is in listening that we can come to believe in the message of the Scriptures, for if we do not take time to listen then other voices will drown out the voice of God.

Thought for the day

Let us take some time for quiet, to find space to listen to God. It is only through listening that our faith will grow.

Prayer

Lord, help my unbelief.
When pressures are strong,
when conflict seems to wreck relationships at home and further away,
help me to take time to listen to you.
Help me to take a step of trust day by day
and so allow me to know you as one who is with me always,
however difficult that day may be.
Amen

Learning to receive forgiveness

Dan 9:4–10; Ps 79; Lk 6:36–38

'Do not judge, and you will not be judged yourselves.'
(Luke 6: 36)

When Jesus told his disciples not to judge, I think he meant the kind of judgement that leads to condemnation and lack of forgiveness of others. He did mean that we should try to be aware of the way things are, to try to assess a situation as accurately as we can, and to judge how we should act. But he did not mean that we should never get angry when we witness injustice or when we become a victim of brutality. Rather, he meant that we should allow compassion to grow in us, to put aside resentment and learn to 'for-give': to give for another in just the same way that God forgives us.

We may struggle to accept the forgiveness of God, but as we receive it becomes easier for us to forgive and in forgiving we know more deeply how God forgives us. The first step in that receiving is to become aware that we are falling short of the way of life shown to us by Jesus in the Gospels. We may even come to realise that, as the early Israelites came to admit, 'we have betrayed your commandments'. Maybe we feel let down, ashamed, discouraged or even on the edge of an abyss. But the path in Lent is one where we learn to receive, to receive the rich store of forgiveness that is in the heart of God for all those who choose to turn again. It is in learning that we need to be forgiven, in learning to receive, that forgiveness becomes easier. Forgiving ourselves is often hardest.

Forgiveness is like the ability to see beyond the action to the inner person who may not even be aware of what they are doing. We are reminded of Christ's own words as he was crucified, 'Father, forgive, for they know not what they do'. Jesus challenges us to forgive, as a matter of priority, for it is through forgiveness that we become able to receive the forgiveness of another, and the forgiveness of God, the greatest gift of all.

Thought for the day

Learning to be forgiven and to forgive is part of treating others as we would want to be treated ourselves.

Prayer

Lord Jesus, help me to face the darker sides of myself,
so I can receive your healing and forgiveness,
for in forgiving myself I can come to forgive others,
and in forgiving others I become more aware of the depth of your forgiveness,
and the freedom that comes from living in your Spirit.
Amen.

Serving

Is 1:10, 16–20; Ps 50; Mt 23:1–12

'The greatest among you must be your servant.'
(Matthew 23:12)

What Jesus is asking for in today's Gospel reading is that those who would be his followers should try to live lives of integrity, to match what they say with what they do. We are reminded here of Christ's own example of washing the disciples' feet at the last supper. Such washing was not just an empty ritual, it was a way of showing those he loved how much our love needs to become expressed in practical, simple action for others. It was a way of expressing the art of noticing the need of those around us, and learning to respond to that need in love.

Who might be those others? Isaiah spells this out more fully. It includes the oppressed, the orphan and the widow; in other words, those at the margins of society. By washing the disciples' feet Jesus was showing what service means in practice, namely, the building up of community life. Community means living out what we say in practical ways, of searching for justice, but not only in words, but through deeds and practical action.

Today we live in a global society, and we are part of a community that does not just include our own immediate neighbours and friends, but extends to the farthest parts of the world. The media bombards us with reports and pictures of natural disasters such as earthquakes and floods, but also with news of famines and wars created by humanity's inhumanity to itself. While part of us may want to block out such images because of their horror, the readings today invite us to face what we fear, to look into the dark side of the global society in which we live. Jesus' actions invite us not only to look, and perceive, but also to act and serve those who are most in need in whatever way we can.

Such small beginnings are the start of a life lived with integrity, one that expresses what the theologian Dietrich Bonhoeffer called 'costly grace' rather than the cheap grace that claims to have faith, but does nothing to show that faith is alive.

Thought for the day

Who am I prepared to serve? Does it include those outside my particular circle of friends and family, those who are different from myself?

Prayer

Lord, teach me to serve as you served,
loving those who were your friends,
but also those who betrayed you.
Help me to come close to those who are different from me,
or excluded from the society I keep.
Teach me to express that solidarity in practical ways
and give me the eyes to see the opportunities before me each day.
Amen

Help us, Lord

Jer 18:18–20; Ps 31; Mt 20:17–28

> *'Release me from the snares they have hidden, for you are my refuge, Lord.'*
>
> (Psalm 30:5)

Those who plotted against Jeremiah resolved to 'hit at him with his own tongue', to twist and use words as a way of silencing the great prophet when he spoke out against their behaviour. Jeremiah felt that he had not been heard; that his enemies had concocted stories against him; that they wanted to catch him out.

One of the deepest pains of all is to know that we are being ignored or dismissed, or that what we have said is being distorted and turned back against us. Jeremiah knew all these difficult and painful emotions. One of the most striking images of 2003 was the sight of a refugee in Britain who had sewed up his eyes and mouth with thread in protest against his treatment as an asylum seeker. Such drastic action gave him and others like him the attention he asked for. The tragedy of his history of abuse and self-mutilation could only stir compassion for one who felt oppression and silencing in the very place where he sought help. He also acted on behalf of others like him, in solidarity with them. Jeremiah had prayed for his enemies, but they continued to abuse him. He then pleaded to God to help him, based on his prayer for them. In this Jeremiah followed the example of all those of faith, who, when they suffer at the hands of others, take their pain to the Lord in prayer.

Praying for those who are hostile towards us is not easy, yet this is the challenge set before us in the readings today. We are called to cry out to the Lord and begin to say, in the midst of conflict, 'I trust in you Lord'. Such experiences of learning to say, 'Help me, Lord' make us more sensitive to others who are in difficult circumstances. God's love is so much deeper than any depth of pain that we might experience. Sometimes the Lord answers through an act of love by another, sometimes we are that vessel of compassion where it is needed. Or perhaps we become aware of the times we ourselves act in oppressive ways, when we are the ones guilty of not letting others speak and be heard. Such awareness, too, can lead to a cry of 'Help me Lord'.

Thought for the day

How often are we afraid to face our own pain or another's pain? Let us have the courage to face the shadow side of others or ourselves and learn to say, 'Help us, Lord'.

Prayer

Lord,
when times are hard,
when I feel vulnerable and oppressed by the things others say or do to me,
help me to learn to ask you for help,
to cry to you in the midst of that pain.
Help me to seek your love and forgiveness
that goes far deeper than I can imagine.
To keep the flame of faith alive in my heart this day.
Amen

Bearing fruit

Jer 17:5–10, Ps 1; Lk 16:19–31

> *'The heart is more devious than any other thing, perverse too: who can pierce its secrets?'*
>
> (Jeremiah 17:9)

For the Hebrews the heart was the seat of the personality, the source of all emotions as well as action, for good or ill. Today we tend to think of the heart in a more limited sense, as the source of our feeling, while we see the head as where we make decisions to act or not to act. If the heart is devious and perverse, then this means we justify particular actions or lack of actions according to our own limited understanding.

The Gospel speaks of the rich man who ignored a poor man called Lazarus. As far as he was concerned Lazarus quite simply was not his problem. He was caught up in what he saw as more important matters: trading, dealing, and making money. But his priorities were all wrong. How often do we justify our own lack of action for the poor by assuming it is someone else who is responsible?

The challenge of the readings today is to take a serious look at what is at the seat of our personality. Are our priorities honouring to God or filled with selfish desires? This is a hard question to answer honestly without the gentle help of the Holy Spirit, who acts like a torch in our inmost self, exposing our true motivations and the real basis for our decisions. Such probing may be uncomfortable, but it ultimately increases our trust in God, and allows us to bear fruit in the way that God intended for us.

The image in the Psalm for today is that of a tree, constantly drawing up the water of life, tapping into the source of that life within the roots of our faith, and allowing that to yield, in time, the fruits of our calling. Such transformation takes time and is a continuous process. We need to learn to be patient with ourselves, to persevere in seeking God with our whole heart and mind even when it seems we are more like dry sticks than flowering branches. But the promise of the readings today is that through faith we can hope that such change is possible, if we stay in touch with God in our innermost being.

Thought for the day

What particular actions can I take in order to meet the needs that I am aware of at the moment?

Prayer

Lord,
forgive my hardness of heart,
my failure to respond to those around me who are in need.
Enable me to draw deeply on your Holy Spirit
so that my life may be filled with plentiful fruit,
fruit that is honouring to you and to your name.
Amen

God's ways

Gen 37:3–4, 12–13, 17–28; Ps 105; Mt 21:33–43, 45–46

> *'It was the stone rejected by the builders that became the keystone'.*
>
> (Matthew 21:42)

Today's readings are about the unexpected, the way God works through surprises and events that seem, at first sight, unlikely or unpromising, at least from a human perspective.

Joseph, the man of dreams, captured by enemies and taken far from those he loved, seemed to have had his dreams dashed to pieces. Yet the grace of God turns his dreaming into reality. But it was not in the way his brothers or Joseph might have expected, for what was a hopeless and terrible situation eventually became a source of blessing and renewal. When events seem to be at a dead end, when all hope is gone, when we experience betrayal, jealously and hatred at the hands of others, God is still at work in spite of such evil intentions. Indeed, it is within such events that we begin to learn about the mercy of God, turning around what seem hopeless and painful events into experiences of love and grace.

This may not necessarily be in such a dramatic way as in the story of Joseph the dreamer. God comes alongside us when we encounter everyday physical, spiritual or mental difficulties. On a national and international scale we can easily call to mind terrible situations and acts of appalling atrocity. Yet no depth of evil or depravity is beyond the reach of God. In situations of injustice, God takes the side of the victim. In Christ, God is taken like a lamb to the slaughter, despised and rejected by the religious authorities of his time. But Christ, like a stone that the builders rejected, becomes the keystone in building up the people of God, through healing love in the Church. God's love can also work through other means as well, through governments, organisations and individuals, who seek to alleviate the pain of those who have suffered at the hands of others. Suffering can, remarkably, serve to sensitise us to the suffering of others.

Thought for the day

How can I become an instrument in the surprise of God, by acting on behalf of one who suffers?

Prayer

Lord Jesus,
you knew the weakness and wickedness of those who plotted against you,
but you knew the love of God is stronger than human hatred,
and the grace of God deeper than human frailty.
When events do not happen according to my hopes,
help me to put my trust in you,
who can turn around and surprise continually,
for God's ways are greater than my ways
and your thoughts greater than my thoughts.
Amen

God is love

Mic 7:14–15, 18–20, Ps 103: 1–4, 9–12; Lk 15:1–3, 11–32

'The Lord is compassion and love.'

(Psalm 103:8)

The prophet Micah asks the Lord to 'tread down our faults to the bottom of the sea', to lay aside that sin which rises to our consciousness in our daily lives, and experience instead the loving forgiveness of God.

God's love is unconditional. It is limitless. Too often we can sense our own striving to please God, like the older brother in the story of the 'prodigal son'. Or maybe we presume that our sin is too great for us still to be worthy to be called 'God's child', like the younger son, who simply wanted to be treated like a servant when he came back home to his father. But the God who is the God of the unexpected is also one who can love in a way that is impossible for human beings, for the depth of God's love and forgiveness is without limit or restraint.

It is hard to understand such love, and Christ told the parable of the lost son in order to illustrate what this love is like. We may find this analogy particularly helpful if our own experience of family love is positive, but few of us will ever have experienced the kind of extravagant love epitomised in this parable. Tuning in to the depth of love that is only possible in God and realising how we are simply at the mercy of One who loves us takes time, but is always there for those who turn towards God in an act of vulnerable openness to grace. The depth of forgiveness possible in God reaches into the heart of our inner being and becomes a place of transformation through the Holy Spirit.

In addition, our vocation or call is to become a mirror of that kind of love and forgiveness, as far as it is possible for us to do so, in our daily lives. Such love and reconciliation is so desperately needed, as we reflect on the lives of our own families and communities, and wider, as we consider the peoples of the struggling nations of the world. Our compassion for the poor and the helpless becomes a mirror of that compassion of God, for it is through human actions that God's love becomes manifest in the world.

Thought for the day

How can I foster a sense of God's love and forgiveness in my own life? How can I show God's compassion to others in a practical way today?

Prayer

Lord, teach me to know more fully the depth and breadth of your love,
to understand that your love and compassion and forgiveness is without limit.
To know that it is through coming to you in openness
that I can know your love and your peace.
Help me to be an instrument of your love and forgiveness in the world.
Teach me today more what it means to become Christ's hands and feet.
Amen.

John Rawsthorne

Third week of Lent

Third Sunday of Lent

At the centre of the story

Ex 3:1–8, 13–15; Ps 103:1–4, 6:8–11; Lk 13:1–9

> *'I have seen the miserable state of my people.'*
>
> (Exodus 3:7)

One of the aspects of the Old Testament that makes things difficult for the modern reader, preoccupied with so-called 'historical' questions, is that the Hebrew people recognised God as the major player in their story, and so they told and re-told that story in ways that highlighted the part that God had played.

Even though enslavement by more powerful nations would be part of their ongoing story and even though the rich and powerful among them would from time to time enslave their own people, they recognised themselves as a freed people and God as their liberator. Moses and the Exodus were the paradigm of their liberation.

Others looking at their story might simply see the usual pattern of a nomad tribal people settling down whenever their travels brought them to a land flowing with milk and honey, where settling down was the obvious thing to do. But as the Hebrew people reflected on their history and recognised their own weaknesses and failures and the dreadful messes they had survived, they knew in their bones that only God could have saved them from themselves, never mind from the depredations of others more powerful than themselves. In case the penny hadn't dropped with everybody, they re-wrote their family history to highlight that fact. 'I have seen the miserable state of my people in Egypt. I have heard their appeal to be free of the slave drivers. Yes, I am well aware of their sufferings. I mean to deliver them out of the hands of the Egyptians and bring them up out of that land to a land rich and broad, a land where milk and honey flow.'

The life, death and resurrection of Jesus complete that liberating work of God. 'And when I am lifted up from the earth, I shall draw all people to myself' (John 12:32). We too recognise ourselves as a liberated people, with a mission to become part of the liberating work of Jesus in the world in which we live. On Easter Day, Jesus said 'As the Father sent me, so am I sending you. After saying this he breathed on them and said: receive the Holy Spirit' (John 20:21–22).

Thought for the day

How would I re-write the story of my life over the past twelve months highlighting God's presence?

Prayer

Lord God
by the power of your Holy Spirit
help me to recognise your presence in the lives of those who work to bring freedom and peace to our world. Amen.

The unity of God's childen

2 Kgs 5:1–15; Ps 42–43; Lk 4:24–30

> *'There were many lepers in Israel, but none of these were cured, except the Syrian, Naaman.'*
>
> (Luke 4:27)

It was a tiny country, identical in size to Wales, constantly threatened by its powerful neighbours, if not subject to them, taken into exile by them, or enslaved by them. So dislike and mistrust of the foreigner was perfectly understandable. The fact that there are so many stories in the Old Testament about good foreigners is a tribute to the core ideals of these people, but they could be very xenophobic.

One of the over-arching themes of the scriptures, both in the Old and the New Testament, is the vision of the unity of all God's children as God's children and therefore as brothers and sisters to each other. Luke presents a Jesus who pushes the boundaries in all directions and in so doing gathers people together around himself, though, as in today's Gospel, there are those who cannot accept it. So the afflicted, the broken-hearted, the captive and those in prison mentioned in Isaiah 61:1–2 are men and women of all peoples without condition.

Pentecost Day brings the languages of the world together, restoring unity out of the confusion of babel. The Acts of the Apostles takes the Church to Rome, gathering people of all sorts along the way. But the struggle to overcome those boundaries of race and religion has always been difficult. Even in the apparently halcyon days of the infant Church, Christians of Jewish and of Jewish-Hellenist backgrounds found it difficult to cope with each other. Luke can say in one breath that 'the whole group of believers was united in heart and soul' (Acts 4:32) and then describe the appointment of Stephen and the other six Hellenists as deacons to minister to the Hellenist Christians because they were feeling badly done to in the daily distribution for widows!

One of the most immediate challenges to us is the arrival of refugees and asylum seekers here on our own doorsteps, many of them not speaking English, from countries with very different customs to our own, and often followers of other faiths, particularly of Islam. Pope John Paul in his 2003 message for the Day for Migrants and Refugees said: 'It (migration) affects millions of human beings and presents a challenge that the pilgrim Church, at the service of the whole human family, cannot fail to take up and meet in the Gospel spirit of universal charity.'

Thought for the day

What influence does my Christian faith have on my attitude to the strangers in our midst?

Prayer

Lord
give me an open heart and generous spirit in my approach to those looking for a new life in our country. Give me the courage to speak with them and for them.
Amen.

Gift and invitation

Dan 3:25, 34–43; Ps 25:4–9; Mt 18:21–25

> *'Treat us gently, as you yourself are gentle and very merciful.'*
>
> (Daniel 3:42)

There are two sides to our encounters with God.

The first and foundational one is God's love for us, pure gift and superabundant in its generosity. The other is the effect that that gift can have on us, forming us into a people who are, so to speak, on God's side in God's love for the world. That is the invitation that comes with the gift!

Peter's question: 'Lord, how often must I forgive my brother if he wrongs me?' introduces a vivid commentary on the Lord's Prayer petition: 'and forgive us our debts as we have forgiven those who are in debt to us' (Matthew 6:12).

God forgives the unforgivable, the huge and impossible-to-repay debt of the first servant. But that forgiving love fails to melt his heart in his dealings with the paltry debt of a fellow human being. God's forgiving love has had no affect on him; he is where he was before his own forgiveness was pronounced, untouched.

Generosity is bound up with forgiveness. Generosity in understanding what has brought this person to the situation where they need forgiveness; generosity in not taking offence to the point of turning away from them; generosity that turns its back on the negativity of the situation; and generosity that can see beyond the present moment to a future that is transformed by an act of forgiveness.

It is fascinating that the word 'debt' is used by Matthew in the Lord's Prayer and that this parable uses the same image where clearly it stands for sin in both cases. We tend to speak of *remitting* debt and *forgiving* sin, but we can easily slip into the language of *forgiving* debt. Perhaps that is our biblical background. The same generosity of spirit is called for in dealing with debt. Our celebration of Jubilee in the year 2000 was a focus on the debilitating effects of both sin and financial debt, as was the Old Testament root from which Jesus took his image. It was a year of forgiving and seeking forgiveness – for sin and for debt. But when Jesus proclaimed 'the year of the Lord's favour', he was not talking about a particular year but about the Jubilee that he brought with him that was to be forever … now and forever.

Thought for the day

'Not seven, I tell you, but seventy-seven times.'

Prayer

Lord
grant me a true spirit of generosity in my forgiveness of
offence and of debt.
Amen.

The closeness of God

Dt 4:1, 5–9; Ps 147; Mt 5:17–19

> *'Indeed, what great nation is there that has its gods so near as the Lord our God is to us whenever we call to him?'*
>
> (Deuteronomy 4:7)

Last night at a local Rotary meeting I gave a talk about some CAFOD partners who I met on a recent visit to Zambia. I spoke for half an hour on a hot summer evening after a good meal in a hotel dining room looking out on to beautiful grounds. A substantial part of the talk was about HIV/Aids and its devastating effect on individuals, families, local communities, on food production, in fact on the whole of life, and on social and political structures.

I described the work of the Home-Based Care Teams in Zambia, with their wonderfully uncomplicated organisation that is so effective in getting personal care, food and medicine to patients in their own homes. Mainly women carers, many have been doing this work voluntarily for more than ten years. The teams can number from 50 to 100 and be caring for many hundreds of patients. Their dedication is extraordinary.

Then this morning I read Moses's words to his people from Deuteronomy: 'Indeed, what great nation is there that has its gods so near as the Lord our God is to us whenever we call to him?' And I wondered, Did I in any way convey that closeness in what I said last night? With all the training and all the provision of food and medicine, with the organisation that lies behind it, it is still most importantly of all the way these carers are with the individuals they look after that finally expresses that closeness of the Lord our God in this moment of need: the concern, the gentleness and tenderness that complement the skills of caring.

As we arrived at one house, a hut in a village in the bush, the young woman patient, desperately ill with Aids, was being placed on a bullock cart to be taken to a clinic a few kilometres away because her needs were now beyond the skills of these carers. But two of the carers lay along side her on the flat bed of the cart to ease the jolting of the journey, an action that spoke volumes about real care and about the closeness of the Lord our God.

Thought for the day

Am I conscious of the closeness of God in my daily life? Does that consciousness affect the way I respond to people?

Prayer

Lord
grant me the grace of knowing that you walk with me every step of the journey.
Amen.

Difficult questions

Jr 7:23–28; Ps 95; Lk 11:14–23

> *' ...some of them said: "It is through Beelzebul, the prince of devils, that he casts out devils".'*
>
> (Luke 4:11–15)

Jesus disturbed people. Not just with his words, but with his actions as well. The taken-for-grantedness of life is upset by stories that question the way things are, by actions that undermine accepted social structures, by deeds that speak of the power of God in a new and different way.

And people react as people do to somebody who asks awkward questions. Some simply reject him because they don't want to have to cope with the questions; some become disturbed because he seems to want to destroy what is important to the way they understand things; others become dangerously angry because he threatens their power base – and they say it is the work of the Devil – while others actually hear the questions and glimpse a new vision of a different world and a new relationship with God and other people.

Our response to what we see or hear is not shaped simply by what we see or hear but by the way in which we see and hear it. Ordinary people could respond rapturously to Jesus, while their leaders could be prompted to seek to kill him ... for the same words or actions. You cannot be more damning than to describe something as the work of the Devil!

Jeremiah, Prophet, sent by God to challenge a people whose behaviour was abominable, was seen as a threat because his challenge hit people whose hearts were closed, who were not listening, who did not want to listen, who were wedded to their ways. They gave Jeremiah a very rough time. It could be very uncomfortable speaking for God. Jesus would find the same, even to the Cross.

Lent is a time for listening – 'this is my Son, the Beloved; he enjoys my favour. Listen to him' (Matthew 17:5). It is a time for honest listening, listening that recognises why some of the sayings or doings of Jesus are not just challenges to us but threats, perhaps to our sense of security, of self-image, of the way we see the Church, or whatever. Honest listening requires Holy Spirit-gifted courage and generosity.

Thought for the day

Listen to my voice, then I will be your God and you shall be my people.

Prayer

Lord
grant me the courage and generosity truly to hear what
you will say to me this day.
Amen.

Why did Jesus die?

Hos 14:2–10; Ps 81; Mk 12:28–34

> *'…which is the first of all the commandments?'*
> (Mark 12:28)

People sometimes point to the Beatitudes or to 1 Corinthians 13 with its Hymn to Love as a description of Jesus himself. Here is another: Jesus is the one who lived the first and second commandments, with all their consequences both wonderful and horrendous.

Why did Jesus die? is one of those questions to which there are just so many answers, answers which all complement each other. But one profoundly true response is that Jesus died because he lived these two commandments in the very real and concrete circumstances of the world in which he lived.

Those who responded to his love, those who recognised it for what it was, were mainly the poor and alienated and outcasts of society. 'Why does he eat with tax collectors and sinners?' asked the scribes of the Pharisees (Mark 2:16). They could equally have asked about the women he chose to speak with, the lepers he touched, the sinners he forgave, the poor to whom he gave hope. From the point of view of the authorities, Jesus was undermining what they stood for and so they had to undermine him, or remove him. They tried on many occasions to undermine his authority, but without success. So they had to remove him. If Jesus had walked away from it all, I wonder would they have pursued him. But Jesus stayed and 'we know love by this, that he laid down his life for us' (1 John 3:16).

Jesus' gift of himself in all things and finally on the Cross was his response to his Father's love for him. Our love is a response to God's love for us. God's love has always been seen in God's actions and Jesus is the culmination of those loving actions.

Which brings us back to 1 John 3:16–17: 'This is the proof of love, that he laid down his life for us – and we ought to lay down our lives for one another. How does God's love abide in anyone who has the world's goods and sees a brother or sister in need and yet refuses to help?'

Thought for the day

Jesus was faithful, to his Father, to us. How am I asked to be faithful in my life? To whom does my faithfulness give life?

Prayer

Lord
I give thanks to you for the gift of so many people
whose faithfulness and generosity inspire and encourage me to continue to walk in your Son's footsteps.
Amen.

The challenge of Lent

Hos 5:15—6:6; Ps 51; Lk 18:9–14

> *'For everyone who exalts himself will be humbled but the man who humbles himself will be exalted.'*
>
> (Luke 18:14)

This is a very Lucan story, vivid and to the point, a story we all know so well. We are not shocked by it. We agree with it. But Jesus's listeners would have been very shocked. The Pharisee was a good member of their religious community who really did fulfil all the observances. The prayer he prayed was a prayer of thanksgiving for what he had received. The tax collector was a man regarded by society as a thief, and a traitor, a man who made his living by defrauding the public through various tricks in the way in which he collected the taxes. Repentance for the tax collector carried very serious consequences for his standard of living - impossible consequences, in fact, because repentance would involve the sort of restitution he could not possibly afford. So his prayer is a prayer of helplessness, even of hopelessness; how can he ever be at rights with God?

Yet Jesus says precisely that this tax collector went home at rights with God! And the Pharisee did not … once again, Jesus turns the accepted order of things on its head.

There are not many repeated sentences in the Gospel, but the last sentence of today's Gospel reading is found also in Luke 14:11 ('for everyone who exalts himself will be humbled but the man who humbles himself will be exalted') and in Luke 1:51-52, at the heart of the Magnificat ('he has routed the arrogant of heart. He has pulled down princes from their thrones and raised high the lowly').

In Lent 2003 Patrick Kelly, Archbishop of Liverpool, wrote: 'The challenge of Lent is this: not to come to the Easter Vigil with our hands full of our good deeds, not even with money raised for those in greatest need. Lent is to bring us fasting, empty handed, thirsting for new life, new birth of water and the Holy Spirit; for things we cannot achieve for and by ourselves.'

'He has come to the help of Israel his servant, mindful of his faithful love – according to the promise he made to our ancestors – of his mercy to Abraham and his descendents for ever' (Luke 1:54-55).

Thought for the day

'Jesus spoke the following parable to some people who prided themselves on being virtuous and despised everyone else.'

Prayer

Lord
help me not to use good deeds to protect myself from
  you and from the needs of your people.
Amen.

Phumzile Zondi

Fourth week of Lent

Fourth Sunday of Lent

Unconditional acceptance

Jos 5:9–12; Ps 35; 2 Cor 5:17–21; Lk 15:1–3, 11–32

> *'My son, you are always with me, and everything I have is yours. But we had to celebrate and be glad, because this brother of yours was dead and is alive again; he was lost and is found.'*
>
> (Luke 15: 31–32)

Awareness–raising workshops on social issues have been difficult in some of our communities because of misunderstandings and lack of information. Many people believe that some problems only belong to certain classes, for example. Gambling is often seen as a problem of the rich, drugs a problem of the poor. HIV/AIDS tends to be seen as a disease of the poor and those who lead immoral lives. These myths have been challenged by inviting people from different social classes and races to come together to share their experiences. This is done with the hope that our communities will become more understanding and supportive.

Our churches are often the most judgemental institutions. Churches always struggle to embrace and accept those who are perceived as different. When they see a link between a person's condition and a presumed contravention of Christian ethics, it results in discrimination, rejection and mistrust.

The father in today's parable challenges his elder son who does not understand why his 'disobedient' younger brother should be given special treatment. The elder brother resents the fact that he has not been rewarded for his obedience.

As activists and as Christians, we should take our lead from the forgiveness and unconditional acceptance of the father in the story, supporting, empowering, crying and rejoicing with those who are suffering or are in 'unacceptable' situations.

Thought for the day

Who am I to judge? Am I perfect?

Prayer

Dear God!
Teach us to love those who are not like us.
Teach us to embrace all those who are suffering.
Help us not to be perpetrators of injustice!
Amen.

Crying brings about healing

Is 65:17–21; Ps 31:2, 4, 5–6, 11–13; Jn 4:43–54

> *'Listen to my cry for help; be not deaf to my weeping . . .'*
> (Psalm 39)

My grandmother has been burying her children and grandchildren one after another. She is 84 years old and does not cry anymore. She believes her tears do not make any difference. She thinks that she has done enough crying in her life and that God may be angry with her. She has shared with me her times of doubting whether God still listens to her. I have also shared with her the times when I feel overwhelmed by all the suffering and injustice in our country. She always has wise words to share that encourage me without fail.

I co-ordinate a campaign on violence against women called the 'Tamar Campaign'. Our title refers to Tamar's story in the Old Testament book of Samuel (2 Samuel 13: 1-21). After being raped Tamar cried out in pain, but her brother Absalom asked her to be silent: 'Be quiet; do not take the matter to heart.' Most survivors of violence share the same story of having being discouraged from crying or even reporting cases of rape or abuse. In our campaign we encourage women to report attacks on them and we ask that the churches openly speak out against all forms of violence. I must say that the churches are not as dismissive of women and children's stories of abuse as they were.

We all go through times of wondering whether we are

doing enough to make this world a better place. Sometimes we think God has given up on us, and does not care anymore. The psalmist captures the rich variety of our human responses to God very well. There are psalms of joy and pain, praise and anger. In some psalms there are doubts as to whether God still listens, in others there is thanksgiving for answers to prayer.

Advocacy and lobbying are forms of crying and weeping. We should continue to find creative ways of crying out in pain, and challenging every kind of discrimination and oppression. And we must always remember that God is on our side. Even though there are times when I doubt it myself, I am committed to encouraging the troubled to cry and weep, because God hears their pleas and sees their tears.

Thought for the day

'A baby that does not cry dies on the mother's back.' (Traditional African saying)

Prayer

Dear God, we pray for the courage
to cry to you
for our needs and of those we love.
Amen.

Never give up

Ezek 47:1–9, 12; Ps 46; Jn 5:1–3, 5–16

> *'I have no one to help me into the pool when the water is stirred. While I am trying to get in, someone goes down ahead of me.'*
>
> (John 5:7)

The sick man in this text 'tried' to get into the pool. This is the key word for me. He had been an invalid for 38 years but he was doing something about it and not just waiting around. Even though he had not succeeded his repeated attempts to get into the pool show that he believed in the power of determination.

Apathy is the greatest disease – even worse than poverty and oppression. There was a time when our communities believed that the bringing of gifts is the best way of showing that one cares. This led to the belief that in times of difficulty God will always send someone to save us.

Once, people in communities (especially African ones) worked together to solve each other's problems. There was always a way out. Nowadays, with the advent of globalization and European civilization, we expect answers to our problems to come from those who are in power. We need to find ways of claiming this power back.

Development practitioners talk about something called 'asset–based approaches to development'. This is just another way of saying that communities should look at what they have and use it to improve their lives. Even if all they possess is a small piece of land, something can planted on it as a step forward. The key is to do something about poverty, starting from where we are.

As Christians, the pain and suffering in the world sometimes overwhelms us. This often leads to a feeling of powerlessness and apathy. Any positive action, no matter how humble, will make a difference in our life. This is the reality of faith. Let us empower communities to discover their own resources!

Thought for the day

The struggle continues. Let us keep trying.

Prayer

Dear God,
we confess that we sometimes lack faith.
and refuse to claim the power freely given to us.
We also confess that we sometimes take power away from others
by rushing to solve their problems for them,
and robbing them of the opportunity to 'try'.
Amen.

Loving the forgotten

Is 49:8–15; Ps 145; Jn 5:17–30

> *'Can a woman forget her baby at the breast, feel no pity for the child she has borne? Even if these were to forget, I shall not forget you.'*
>
> (Isaiah 49:15)

'I managed to hide my HIV–positive status from my mother for three years. It was difficult. She kept on asking me what was wrong with me. A lot of money was wasted on trying to appease our ancestors. My parents believed my sickness was a curse from the spirit world. I could not challenge their beliefs. I knew exactly what would happen to me if I told them the truth. I was forgotten in the process. Finding a solution became my mother's number one priority. Then our neighbour, who is a nurse, told my mother the truth, thinking she was doing us all a favour. I was asked to take all my things and leave. I was told I had brought shame and disgrace to the family. Fortunately one of my aunts gave me shelter and a lot of support. If it was not for her, I would be dead today.'

When one looks at Sindi it is difficult to believe her story. She is very positive about life even though her parents have disowned her. She believes her parents rejected her due to ignorance, a lack of understanding about her illness. They know where she lives, but will not have anything to do with her.

Unfortunately, communities of Christians have not

behaved very differently. Although this is slowly starting to change, people who are living with HIV/AIDS do not feel welcome in our churches. There has been a lot of 'judgemental and hate speech'. People with HIV/AIDS are forgotten, nobody visits them and some of them are not even buried by their own ministers. When people come to our churches and the numbers grow, we rejoice. But when the same people feel alienated and leave, nobody bothers. More often we assume that they are guilty.

In support groups for AIDS sufferers we constantly remind ourselves that God is always with us, does not judge us and cares for us. We know that God does not forget us, even when everyone else has.

During Lent when we celebrate the sacrifice that was made for us, it is important to remember in a special way those who are despised and rejected. May we learn to sacrifice with our time by going out of our way to find them and make them feel part of the Body of Christ.

Thought for the day

The forgotten and despised need us the most.

Prayer

God, Our Creator,
may most of our time
be given to those who need to know and feel your love
and acceptance.
May we learn from the Good Shepherd,
to look for the lost and forgotten.
Amen.

What is rightfully ours

Ex 32:7–14; Ps 106; Jn 5:31–47

> *'Why should the Egyptians say, "It was with evil intent that he brought them out, to kill them in the mountains and to wipe them off the face of the earth?" Turn from your anger; relent and do not bring disaster on your people.'*
>
> (Exodus 32:12)

'If I do not steal it means I have to sleep without a meal. I do not steal from the poor, I only take from those who have too much. Now you tell me what's wrong with that,' said a young person who lives on the streets. This is called 'claiming back what is rightfully ours.' This young person is always in trouble with the law and this makes him very angry because he does not believe he should be punished for fulfilling his needs in a 'decent' way.

God's name was used by many in South Africa to justify apartheid and the unequal distribution of resources. Even the robbing of people was done coupled with blessings pronounced in God's name. The end to all the oppressive practices came about with promises of compensation and redress from the new government. Seeing so little change in their lives people feel justified in taking it upon themselves to restore what was stolen from them.

The Exodus story is known as a story of liberation. The oppressed in my country repeatedly claim that they can identify with the experiences of the Israelites. Even after the political liberation that was promised to end economic oppression, they feel the old oppressors are still mocking them. The economic oppression has led to other problems, such as the high rate of crime, disease and death. It is the poor and oppressed that are the victims of all these social ills. The rich constantly introduce new rules and systems for their own benefit, and get richer each day.

In the face of all this pain and suffering, people are told that some of these things are punishment from God. 'These are the signs of God's wrath,' some say. Why would God punish the wrong people? If God is angry, then that anger is displaced.

During this time, let us spread the message of hope and life. Let us not use fear tactics and tell people that God is punishing them, when we should be naming the real culprits.

Thought for the day

The eyes of the Lord are on those who fear him ...
to deliver them from death
and keep them alive in famine.

(Psalm 33:18, 19)

Prayer

Dear God,
teach us to speak the truth in love.
Let us face all our enemies,
with the assurance that you are on our side,
and evil systems will come to an end.
Amen.

New Songs

Wis 2:1, 12–22; Ps 34; Jn 7:1–2, 10:25–30

> *'Sing to him a new song . . . and shout for joy.'*
> (Psalm 33:3)

In my own journey with the HIV virus this has been my favourite motto. This virus is seen as a killer. This is what we are told when we first find out that we are infected. When I say 'we', I am referring to all those people who have come to terms with their infection and have turned this enemy into an ally.

Most conferences, seminars and workshops on HIV/AIDS that I have attended all teach and speak about this condition as the greatest enemy. I always make it a point to challenge some of the speakers to try and understand the virus from the perspective of the person living with HIV/AIDS. There comes a time when one has to choose between being scared and debilitated by it, or befriending it. You find a way of living together amicably. In the midst of all the old and depressing songs that were sung about HIV/AIDS, I chose to look for a new song that has helped me to remain positive about life.

All the pain and suffering that comes with the virus can be the motivation to seize every moment. Instead of giving in to the disease, one can use it as a stepping stone. It has made me realise how important every opportunity is.

This is the song we should sing together. A song of

hope, life and survival should be sung in our sermons and our newspapers. We must find ways of enhancing this message instead of just fighting the virus. It is high time that even when people living with HIV/AIDS are expected to sing the old songs, we encourage the infected and affected to sing new songs. This is not easy but, with our support and prayers, it is possible.

This is one of my favourite choruses:

> I will celebrate, sing unto the Lord
> I will sing to God a new song.
> I will praise God.
> I will sing to God a new song.

Thought for the day

'Do not let any unwholesome talk come out of your mouths, but only what is helpful for building others up according to their needs. That it may benefit those who listen.'

(Ephesians 4: 29)

Prayer

Dear God
may we speak joy into being even where there is sorrow;
may we speak life into being even where there is death.
Amen

Committed to life for all

Jer 11:18–20; Ps 7; Jn 7:40–52

> *'Let me see your vengeance upon them, for to you I have committed my cause.'*
>
> (Jeremiah 11:18–20)

Most churches still do not fully understand the meaning of Jesus' words in John 10: 10. Eighty per cent of lay people in our churches are women but there is less than ten per cent of women within the church who are given opportunities to lead. The language that the churches use is often sexist and constantly reminds women that they are inferior. Women are hardly ever given space to voice their spirituality neither are they encouraged to challenge some of the male–dominated teachings.

Women have to fight for recognition as human beings both inside and outside the church. Texts about women are hardly ever read, if they are, it is usually to prove how 'weak' they are. The fact that Jesus had women disciples is unheard of, especially during services.

Women who have taken it upon themselves to openly challenge church leaders are labelled, discriminated against, alienated and sometimes rejected. Jeremiah said things he 'should not have said', and this made him an enemy. But because he was doing this for a just cause, God protected him.

Those of us who believe in the equality of all believers should continue to speak out and educate all the churches. We should see to it that our words bring life to all. God's grace and mercy is not for the chosen few but for all those who claim it.

Thought for the day

We are all created in the image of God and Jesus came so that we may have life in abundance.

Prayer

God
who stands with us in our fight against discrimination
   and injustice
protect us and give us courage
to continue with our call
for respect and the recognition of women.
Amen.

Joseph Donders

Fifth week of Lent

Fifth Sunday of Lent

On not drawing a line

Is 43:16–21; Ps 126; Ph 3:8–14; Jn 8:1–11

> *'If there is one of you who has not sinned, let him be the first to throw a stone at her.'*
>
> (John 8:7)

That morning Jesus did not agree with the people around him. They had been doing the simplest thing in the world. Something so simple, that we are doing it all the time. They had been drawing a divisive line between the good ones and the evil ones. They were good, and the woman was bad, no longer worthy to live.

She had been caught in the act of adultery. Something you cannot do on your own. Yet she was the only one they pushed in front of him. She was unclean, a sinner, and they were the ones standing in for the law, for purity and integrity.

Jesus did not even look up at them. He remained sitting, drawing with his finger some lines in the sand: crosses, circles, triangles. They tried to force him to take sides. They asked him, 'Moses has ordered us in the Law to condemn women like this to death by stoning. What have you to say?'

He did not answer them, but when they persisted, he finally looked up and even then, he did not answer their question at all. He asked them his question. 'Who among you is without sin?' How could they draw that line around her? Put her in a circle? Did they not realise that they belonged in that circle, too? Finally, they did, and they left the scene, one by one, the older ones first.

It is a story so simple that it repeats itself all the time. How often do we divide the people around us into the good ones and the bad ones? We belong to the good ones, they to the bad ones. How often do we frustrate, boycott and sabotage each other because of that line. But Jesus says, 'That line is a lie. It will be no help in the world you want to restore. All of you are co–responsible for the world as it is. You all have to change your ways, and to sin no more.'

It is what he told the woman, and, by implication, all of them, and all of us.

Thought for the day

'For when the One Great Scorer comes, to write against your name,
He marks – not that you won or lost, but how you played the game.'

(Grantland Rice, 1880–1954)

Let us pray

Loving God,
as we grow older help us to live in peace.
Help us to do what is just,
as responsible members of the body of your Son,
our Lord and Brother Jesus Christ. Amen.

Our family table

Dan 13:1–9, 15–17, 19–30; Ps 23; Jn 8:12–20

'You do not know me, nor do you know my father!'
(John 8: 19)

She was a foreigner in the country where he studied. She was a stranger not only because of the far–off country she came from, but also because of her religious beliefs. A faith that was obvious to everyone, if only because of the way she was dressed.

She was carrying a food tray in the university cafeteria. People were sitting at every table. There were still a few empty places, but she hesitated to take one. Yet she could not just stand there, so she decided to sit down at one of the tables. When she did, she was told that she was not welcome. They told her that the table was only for people of their kind and their religious conviction. She could not sit with them, and they could not sit with her.

Is this an exaggerated story? No, it happens regularly all over the world in all kinds of circumstances. Bigoted religionists of all kinds are often the perpetrators. They do it in the name of their religious convictions. It is in the name of God and their relation to God that they demand segregation.

It is an attitude that is the precise opposite of Jesus' conviction and teaching. Jesus says: 'You do not know me, nor do you know my Father; if you did know me, you would know my Father as well.' Having that one

Parent means that there is only one family table, a common table, to which all are welcome. A table filled with all we need. It is because of that table that Jesus reached out beyond himself to all that exist. If we are true to ourselves, we should do the same, since we are of his Spirit.

Understanding what it means to reach out to God, the source of our common being, we would reach out to all other human beings, and even to the rest of creation. Look around you wherever you happen to be today, and embrace in spirit humans, animals, plants, and everything around you. You will be dancing with God.

Thought for the day

' "There is communion of more than our bodies when bread is broken and wine is drunk." And that is my answer when people ask me: "Why do you write about hunger . . . ?" '

(M.F.K. Fisher 1908–1992)

Let us pray

Father,
give us today our daily bread.
And teach us how to share it at one table for all.
Amen.

Impatience and patience

Num 21:4–9; Ps 102; Jn 8:21–30

'On the way the people lost patience . . .'

(Numbers 21:5)

The Bible is a book full of stories. There are hundreds, maybe thousands of them. These stories cover all possible human situations. They tell about very holy and mystical moments, moment of 'epiphanies', sudden manifestations of God in the midst of common human affairs. And there are also stories about betrayal and crime, about the dark side of human affairs.

The story today is about a lack of patience. On their way out of Egypt, the people became edgy. They complained bitterly. They were fed up with the desert. They were tired of all the marching. They could not bear the dry rations they received, and they hated the lack of water.

In their impatience they started to have doubts about Moses, and his leadership. Finally they even turned against God.

It is all rather commonplace. It is all very human. When difficulties surround us, when things do not develop as we would like them to, notwithstanding our efforts and good intentions, rebellion is in the air. Where is God? Is this what we deserve after all we did?

These thoughts are like the serpents that threatened the Isrealites in the desert. They poison our relations with our self, with others, and with God. We become sarcastic and cynical, sneaky and mean. And the longer the journey, the more inhospitable the world becomes.

In their frustration they turned to Moses, who notwithstanding their complaints about his leadership, interceded for them. They got their answer. They were asked to make a bronze serpent and put it on a standard. (It is the same emblem you sometimes see today used by doctors and medical institutions.) Seeing it, they were invigorated and healed, regaining faith in their promised future.

Now, centuries later, in this season of Lent we are asked to look at Jesus on his standard, the cross. We are asked to look up at him, to see what the world did to him. Looking at him, whom we believe is risen, we learn that the patience shown on that cross won all the life to come.

Thought for the day

'Let nothing disturb thee, nothing afright thee. All things are passing, God never changeth.'

(Teresa of Avila 1515–82)

Prayer

Lord,
teach me to be patient
even when my plans seem thwarted
and my projects have collapsed.
Do not let the storm of my impatience overcome me,
but stretch out your hand and calm me.
Amen.

On being free

Dan 3:14–20, 24–28, 52–56; Jn 8:31–42

> *'So if the Son makes you free, you will be free indeed.'*
> (John 8: 36)

One of the striking things about Jesus is that there was nothing that would stop him from doing God's will. He first showed this freedom as a child. Luke tells us that on a pilgrimage to Jerusalem with his parents he stayed in the temple, to the great distress of Mary and Joseph. Once they had found him, Mary reprimanded him saying, 'My child, why have you done this to us? See how worried your father and I have been looking for you.'

'Why were you looking for me?' Jesus replied, 'Did you not know that I must be busy with my Father's affairs?' (Luke 2:48).

Luke then adds that after this Jesus went home with his parents and that he lived 'under their authority'. Yet one thing had become clear: even family bonds would not keep him from doing what his Father asked him to do. Nothing was going to hold him back. Jesus sets us an example here, as he always does. But he does more than that. He shows us the freedom that each one of us, too, is capable of.

In 1971 Pope Paul VI wrote a letter about social justice. In it he explained the price we have to pay to attain this freedom: 'This liberation starts with the interior freedom that [we] must find again with regard to [our] goods and our powers; [we] will never reach it except through a genuine readiness to serve' (*Octagesimo Adveniens*, 45).

Mother Teresa of Calcutta put it in an different way, when she was interviewed on the way of life of her Little Sisters of the Poor: 'We have very little, so we have nothing to be preoccupied with. The more you have, the more you are occupied, the less you give. But the less you have, the freer you are. Poverty for us is a freedom' (*Time*, 29 December 1975).

The more you have, the more security you need, the less truly free you are. This is becoming increasingly obvious in the modern world, for individuals and for nations. Let us pray that the freedom Jesus realised in his life may help us to free ourselves.

Thought for the day

'Riches and power are but gifts of blind fate, whereas goodness is the result of one's own merits.'

(Héloise 1098–1164)

Prayer

Almighty and ever loving God,
you put the seed of freedom in our hearts.
Help may us to make our choices in the way your Son Jesus did.
Amen.

Seeing Abraham and Sarah

Gen 17:3–9; Ps 105; Jn 8:51–59

'You are not fifty yet, and you have seen Abraham?'
(John 8:57)

In the northern part of the Netherlands, Friesland or Frisia, local tradition interprets this saying of the gospel reading of today in a curious way. A remark made with the intent of ridiculing Jesus – 'You are not fifty yet and you have seen Abraham?' – has been taken up in their local folklore as a tradition that you will 'see Abraham' when you are fifty. People who reach that age receive on their birthday a doll made of bread dough baked in the form of Abraham, if they are men; and of Sarah if they are women. It is a custom that has now spread all over the Netherlands and Belgium. The dolls are no longer only made of bread, they are sometimes life–size dolls made of paper and all kinds of other material.

Strictly, this interpretation of the biblical text does not make much sense. The people around Jesus wanted to mock him. And yet this ancient folklore might point at a deeper insight worth considering. 'Seeing Abraham and Sarah' confronts us with the mission that God entrusted to these ancestors of ours. They were called out of an ancient pagan culture to start a journey. A journey that would lead them to a new future, a different human situation, a better homeland, a heavenly one, a lasting city, with God as its architect and maker.

Abraham, Sarah and their descendants would be

blessed when they would remain faithful to their call. But that blessing was not going to be restricted to them. Through them, all the nations of the earth would be blessed. 'All the tribes of the earth shall bless themselves by you' (Genesis 12: 3).

Abraham and Sarah are the first ones who responded to God's plan of a 'restoration of this world', 'to gather together in unity the scattered children of God' (John 11:52). It is this insight, this wisdom, that our day and age needs to assure a sane and God–willed globalisation. It would be a good thing if all of us would be able to 'see Abraham and Sarah', even long before we are fifty!

Thought for the day

'Justice is like the Kingdom of God. It is not without us as a fact, it is within us as a great yearning.'

(George Eliot 1819–80)

Prayer

Jesus,
you who died 'to gather together in unity the scattered children of God'
and who dreamed of getting us together at the table of your Father,
bless all those who are engaged in that work.
Amen.

All of you

Jer 20:10–13; Ps 18; Jn 10:31–42

> *'Is it not written in your Law: I said, you are gods!'*
> (John 10:34)

No one likes to be overlooked and not to count. Toddlers surrounded by adults too busy to pay attention to them will start to act up to draw their attention. When they are a little older they might ask in the middle of the conversation at table, 'Why does no–one talk to me?'

All of us, young and old, dislike being ignored. Don't you dislike being served in a shop or at a post office by someone who at the same time is talking on the phone to someone else, hardly bothering to pay attention to you?

Jesus was not exactly overlooked by the people who challenged him on his relationship with God. They laughed at him. They did not only scorn him, they even wanted to kill him as a blasphemer, a nobody. It is then that Jesus makes a statement, not only about his own special relationship with God, but more generally on the way each of us relates to God.

He said: 'Is it not written in your Law: I said, you are gods? So [the Law] uses the word "gods" of those people to whom the word of God was addressed – and scripture cannot be set aside.'

Jesus was referring to Psalm 82:6, where we read:

I once said,
'You too are gods,
children of the most high,
All of you.'

No one should be overlooked. No one should be neglected. Every person counts. We are all created in the image of God. God's life–giving breath is what gives life to all of us. There is the story about a little girl who asked her grandfather, 'Where does God live?' Her grandfather lifted her up above the water of a nearby creek, and asked her, 'Look down in the water and tell me what you see.' 'I see myself,' the little girl said. 'That is where God lives,' said the old man, 'God lives in you'.

Making this truth about us real is the work of justice. Seeking justice, loving mercifully, walking humbly, treating each person as though she or he were yourself, is what all this is about. The world has to be made new. It is the reason Jesus joined us.

Thought for the day
'There is that of God in everyone.'

(Quaker saying)

Prayer
Almighty God,
help me to be aware of the presence of your Breath
and your life–giving Spirit
not only in myself,
but in all of humanity.
Let it become more and more the guiding star in my life.
Amen.

Gathering

Ezek 37:21–28; Jer 31:1–13; Jn 11:45–56

> *'Jesus was to die for the nation, but not for the nation only, but to gather together in unity the scattered children of God.'*
>
> (John 11:52)

We all know what can happen in the telling of a story. Someone is hurt in an accident. He comes home. He is asked to tell what happened to him. He can't tell it as yet. He says, 'Ask me later, I need a rest.'

The following day he tells the story, again and again. It is as if he needs to tell it, to get rid of the shock the accident caused. Telling the story he begins to understand how to tell it. He stresses some details and omits others. The more often the story is told the shorter it gets. After some time it can be told in a few words.

Something like that happened to the salvation story. Telling it again and again, it often got reduced to three elements: Fall, Redemption, and Life hereafter. Or, to put it in a few words: Jesus died for our sin to save us from hell.

The problem with this reduced version is not that it is untrue. It is true. The difficulty is that it does not offer the full picture. During the days before his crucifixion Jesus prayed 'That they may be one' twice: John 17:11 and 17: 22. This prayer that adds a new perspective too often overlooked in our conventional piety. We see this perspective in today's gospel reading. Caiaphas had called a meeting to decide what to do about Jesus. So many people had begun to follow Jesus that the situation risked running out of hand. The meeting was afraid of a looming catastrophe. It is then that Caiaphas said:

'It is better for one man to die for the people than for the whole nation to be destroyed.'

John adds: 'He did not speak in his own person, it was as high priest that he made this prophecy, that Jesus was to die for the nation, and not for the nation only, but to gather in unity the scattered children of God.' Unwittingly, Caiaphas had described the mission of Jesus, and consequently of us, his disciples! We are 'gatherers', bringing the family of God together.

Thought for the day

'In essential things – unity; in unimportant things – freedom; in all things – charity.'

(Pope John XXIII, 1881–1963)

Prayer

Jesus,
lead us to be tolerant and understanding of others,
looking for what unites people rather than what might divide and separate.
Inspire us to build your reign in our world today.
Amen.

Wendy M. Wright

Holy Week and Easter Sunday

Passion Sunday

An upside–down God

Is 50:4–7; Ps 22; Ph 2:6–11; Lk 22:14—23:56

> '... *Yet he did not cling to his equality with God but emptied himself to assume the condition of a slave* ...'
> (Philippians 2:6b–7a)

It is all upside–down. It is not what we expect. It begins with the triumphal parade. The cheering crowds. We expect him on a snorting steed; his chiselled profile that of a conquering hero. Instead, he arrives on a timid donkey. We follow him into Jerusalem and assemble with the rest in an upper room for the Passover Supper. He is enigmatic as he breaks the bread and passes it, promising us some sort of kingdom. Some of us quarrel about who is the greatest among us. He surprises us all: it is those who serve who are the greatest. It is all upside–down.

He seems restless and withdraws apart. We are tired and troubled but drift out after him, finding soft crevices on the Mount where we curl up to rest. Suddenly, he appears, face stained with sweat and blood. Behind him, armed men menace. We take up our swords to fend them off. Leave off! He commands us. They drag him away in disgrace. The inexorable machine of condemnation cannot be stopped. He is tried, humiliated, mutilated, dies. It is all upside down. It is not what we expected.

What does it mean to be a disciple of this man? In our modern world, it is the winners, the powerful who are the heroes. Dominance on the world stage is measured by military strength, by a nation's capacity to control through force. All over the world, the default mode is violence. In families and in communities, dominance is maintained by intimidation. We resist seeing ourselves in anyone who is 'other', anyone who is not just like us. And we want to erase them. We persist in living as though it is power – usually won through violence – that will guarantee us the fullness of life.

To follow this man means unlearning every instinct, every knowing that we have lived with so far. It's not about victory over others. It's not about winning. It is about living into the mystery of the kingdom that, with his life and his death, he proclaimed. The greatest among us are not the powerful who are served but those who serve. We are admonished to put down our swords. He does not rule by force or by conquest. This is not his way. It is not what we expected.

Thought for the day

'The great historical event, the coming of the kingdom, is made clear and is "realized" in proportion as Christians themselves live the life of the Kingdom in the circumstances of their own time and place.' (Thomas Merton)

Prayer

Gracious God,
In this holiest of weeks lead us gently in your way.
Unlearn us. Let us be content to serve.
Stay our hands as we reach for the sword.
Give us your heart so that we will cease to fear your upside down way. Amen.

For what are we formed?

Is 42:1–7; Ps 27; Jn 12:1–11

> *'I have taken you by the hand and formed you.'*
> (Isaiah 42:6)

It is break week at the University and I have carried my bag lunch over to the gymnasium where the Nebraska Annual Special Olympics is taking place. I have always loved the event and felt it as a respite from the ungenerous competitiveness of academia. I settle myself on a low bench to enjoy the festivities. As I do, I pick up a flyer that reports the result of an international survey. It reads:

'For decades, many have believed that the doors to inclusion of individuals with intellectual disabilities in mainstream society have been shut tight because of misconceptions, ignorance and fear. Now, those suspicions have scientific validation, according to a groundbreaking study released today by Special Olympics. Overall, the survey shows that the general population lacks an appreciation of the range of capabilities of individuals with intellectual disabilities, and therefore have low expectations of how much people with mental disabilities can achieve. The study also revealed that the world still believes individuals with intellectual disabilities should work and learn in separate settings, apart from people without disabilities.'

The facility is crowded with excited participants, their coaches, families and caregivers. In the hall to my left, the atmosphere is joyful: the winner of a weightlifting competition is glowing. He is being surrounded by his competitors and congratulated with a group hug. Their shared joy is infectious.

In his retelling of the Jesus story, Luke has the young carpenter from Galilee inaugurate his public ministry in a surprising way. He stands up in the synagogue and proclaims jubilee. He reaches down into the wellspring of an ancient prophetic tradition and draws up the image of that seven–times–seven–year celebration during which the just community is to be restored: when land will be redistributed, debts forgiven, and prisoners freed. He trumpets the advent of God's own shalom. The wounded, the lost, the blind, and the lame: all will be restored to wholeness. This same proclamation resounds this Monday of Holy Week.

It is this shalom for which we were formed. It is this shalom – this kingdom – that Mary of Bethany, kneeling at Jesus' feet and anointing them, acknowledged. Created in the image and likeness of God, we are designed for the fullness of life. We are shaped to the contours of the Kingdom. Not simply as individuals, each by him– or herself, but together. We are made, all of us, for our shared joy.

Thought for the day

'We must be saved together. We must come to God together. Together we must all return to our Father's house. What would God say to us if some of us came to him without the others?' (Charles Peguy)

Prayer

We are formed for this, God of Goodness, for your shalom. We are shaped for your kingdom.

Teach us to be your community of love. Help us to live into our shared joy. Amen.

Who hears my cry?

Is 49:1–6; Ps 71; Jn 13:21–33, 36–38

> *'Oh come and rescue me God, Yahweh come quickly and help me.'*
>
> (Psalm 70:1)

It is an image I cannot shake. It lives inside me like some dark secret consigned to oblivion until it surfaces, unbidden on a sunny summer afternoon. Strangely, the image came to me in the form of the printed word: a newspaper notice. It was the mid–eighties, I had come into the empty common room of the seminary where my husband was enrolled as a student and idly picked up a copy of the *Boston Globe*. An article on an inside page caught my eye. The dateline was Central America. As I read, the horror of the scene unfolds inside me. A high plain, open to the sky. Government aircraft patrol overhead, scanning the terrain for signs of guerrilla activity. Movement is sighted, the aircraft descend swiftly toward the open plane, their arsenals yawn open, and the strafing begins, hurtling projectiles earthward. The ground convulses, sending columns of spiralling dust skyward. On the ground, a young peasant woman with two young children hears the approaching thunder. Frightened, she runs, runs, as fast as she can toward the shelter of a nearby grove of trees, one baby bouncing on her hip, the other child dragging behind. Panting, running, she becomes aware that she cannot reach the grove in time and so she stops abruptly, huddles the children together in front of her, and covers them, draping her own body above them to form a human canopy. Later, when the aircraft have left the area, villagers find the three inert forms in this same deep, instinctive gesture of maternal protection.

Who will cry out for the women and the children, the old men, the boys, caught in the violence of civil unrest? Who will cry out as the powerful nations of the world protect their interests by selling weapons around the world. Who will cry out for those caught in the middle? Who will dare to imagine new ways to resolve conflict, dream of imagining and working for a world where violence, greed, hatred, ignorance, apathy, and lust for power do not rule the day?

Jesus' cry, his loneliness on this painful march through Jerusalem, is echoed over and over in countless languages on countless unsheltered plains all over the world. Who will hear?

Thought for the day

'The poor are the constant cry that denounces not only social injustice but also the scant generosity of our own church. The poorer you are the more you possess the reign of God, provided you truly live that spirituality.' (Oscar Romero)

Prayer

God of the poor, the lost, the vulnerable,
may we hear their cries as you do.
May we become the sacred canopies that shelter and protect them.
Amen.

A disciple's ear

Is 50: 4–9; Ps 69; Mt 26:14–25

> *'Each morning he wakes me to hear, to listen like a disciple.'*
>
> (Psalm 50: 4b)

The scene is one of foreboding. He senses that among his dearest friends is one who will not only abandon him but who will betray him. He will be handed over – out of fear, disappointment, a misplaced sense of justice, malice, greed, a lack of empathy, who knows? Does it matter? The betrayal will be applauded by those who wish to keep order, condoned by the crowds, sealed by religious and civil authority. This condemned man is the one who stood with such authority on the Mount and spoke to us a new law: 'Love your enemies and pray for those who persecute you.' 'Do not return evil for evil but return evil with good.' We seemed to listen then. Did we?

It is five minutes to midnight. In the upper window of the state penitentiary the dark outline of a man appears against the glare of florescent lights. He seems to pause momentarily and look out at the crowds assembled below. We are below, on the right of the barricade that separates the two assembled factions. We stand silently, hands stuffed in our jackets, scarves wound around our necks to keep out the night chill and pray. A few of us sing quietly, hymns that spontaneously well up from our grief, their voices all but drowned by the harsh sounds issuing from the crowd surging on the other side of the barricade. Those gathered there laugh and hoot and throw streamers. 'Fry Willy!' they chant, 'Fry Willy!' A few young men hoist blond–haired co–eds up on their shoulders. The girls giggle and wave their arms. Not all of those gathered across the barricade are in such a festive mood. They appear stern and dignified. They carry placards that read: 'All are subject to the law.' 'The guilty must be punished.'

The countdown begins. We bow our heads and pray for God's mercy. 'Five, four, three, two, one,' the frenzied shout pulses up to our left. 'Fry Willy!!' We read next day in the newspaper that the first attempt at executing the condemned prisoner failed, that the circuits of the electric chair had to be repaired. On the second try, the sentence passed by the authorities was successfully carried out.

Thought for the day

'Jesus also admonished his followers to love their enemies and to pray for them that despitefully used them . . . Their lives had been conditioned to seek redress in the time–honoured tradition of retaliation. Yet Jesus taught them that only through a creative love for their enemies could they be children of their father in heaven and also that love and forgiveness were absolute necessities for spiritual maturity.' (Martin Luther King, Jr)

Prayer

Wake me, God.
Wake me again this morning.
Open my eyes to the possibilities of this new day.
Open my ears to the music of your forgiveness.
Teach the song of your mercy.
Inscribe its melody in my heart. Amen.

The example

Ex 12:1–8, 11–14; Ps 116; 1 Co 11:23–26; Jn 13:1–15

> *'I have given you an example so that you may copy what I have done for you.'*
>
> (John 13:15)

It is so simple. Yet we complicate it so. One gesture. He wraps a towel around his waist, pours water in a basin. He kneels. He washes his friends' feet. Then he queries them: Do you understand what I have done? I have given you an example. So should you do.

Tall, slender, poised, she stands on the stage at the awards ceremony. Each year we graduate a number of Theology majors: some become secondary teachers, some launch into ministry, some pursue medical or dental studies or practice law. But she has a clear vision of the distinctive path she will follow. Her award citation is read aloud. She will head to medical school and plans on becoming a medical missionary. The dean recalls her summer service in an African leper colony and the time when she was called upon to use her skills at midwifery by delivering a baby in an aircraft flying over Angola.

After the ceremony I head to the gymnasium to take an afternoon jog, all the celebration having worn me out. The trajectory of my middle–aged life is very much in mind as I reflect on our students. Delivering a baby over Angola! Serving in a leper colony! Well, I think, if there's ever going to be an accounting of the grand ways we've served one another, I'm going to be at the end of the line.

One of the women on the cleaning staff comes around the corner of the row of lockers. We usually chat when I'm here. She regales me with the progress of a knee injury, and boasts about how many boxes of Girl Scout Cookies her niece recently sold. I tell her I miss my son, who is off on a camping trip. We shake our heads together in dismay as she recounts how, at the spring luncheon for all the University staff, the custodians were required to stay after they ate and work. 'Imagine that, we're asked to dinner then told to clean up after ourselves!' Because of her, I am aware that I share a living space with people who experience it quite differently than either my colleagues or I do.

Perhaps my résumé, if I were to construct such a one, might be made to include some lines that could qualify as heroic service. And Jesus' example, toweling his friends' feet, urges me to stretch beyond my present comfort zone. But I'm reminded that service takes different forms. Wherever we are, we can copy something of the spirit of that gentle, kneeling gesture.

Thought for the day

'Only he who has learned to love men one by one reaches, in his relation to heaven, God as the God of all the world ... For he learns to love the God of the universe, only in the measure in which he himself learns to love the world.' (Martin Buber)

Prayer

You have wrapped the towel firmly around your waist.
You have knelt before us, your basin of cool water
  lapping to refresh our tired feet.
Teach us to do the same. Amen.

The hope to which we are called

Is 52:13—53:12; Ps 31; Heb 4:14–16, 5:7–9; Jn 18:1—19:42

> *'One of the soldiers pierced his side with a lance; and immediately there came out blood and water.'*
>
> (John 19:34)

The early fathers of the church picked out and seized upon one striking detail from the Johannine narrative of the passion. The account tells us that as Jesus' lifeless body hung from the cross, one of the soldiers, presumably to test if some life remained, punctured the flesh. Out poured blood and water. This, the fathers said, represents the church, the mystical body of Christ. From it pours an ever–fresh fountain: the waters of baptism and the saving blood of the Eucharist. At the heart of the universe lies this grace–filled secret that never ceases to astonish us: from ending, beginning, from despair, hope, from death, new life.

It was a Good Friday like no other. Our via dolorosa was not the well–trod pilgrim way in the Holy Land but a sobering trek through the crowded streets of Port–au–Prince, Haiti. From the squalor of Citi Soleil, where more than ten thousand human beings squat in a waterless encampment under the blazing Caribbean sun, to the churches where the blood of those who have been killed for the cause of Haitian democracy lies fresh on the doorposts, to the decrepit AIDs hospice where women and small children lay dying, I walked the way of the Haitian peoples' sorrow.

Outside the church of Saint John Bosco, embedded in a low concrete wall, are a row of lambi, the conch shells which are the liberating symbol of the long ago slave revolution that made Haiti the first free black republic in the world. The lambi alongside the church speak only in part of a political ideal. They speak as well with profoundly religious overtones. In this current desolation, the gleaming conch shells witness to the hope that sustains the Haitian people; a mysterious hope that vitalizes what to an outsider seems a hopeless situation. This is a hope that life will emerge out of death, a hope that is neither wishful thinking nor some vague expectation of an afterlife. This is a hope for the fullness of life. It is the hope to which we are all called.

Thought for the day

'When we suffer, we are told we suffer with Christ . . . We suffer his loneliness and fear in the garden when his friends slept. We are bowed down with him under the weight of not only our own sins but also the sins of each other, of the whole world. We are those who are sinned against and those who are sinning. We are identified with him, one with him. We are members of his mystical body. (Dorothy Day)

Prayer

You, whose death promises us Life,
may we never take the terrible mystery of this Good Day
for granted.
May we never cease to hope with the expansiveness
with which we are called. Amen

Rolling the stone

Gen 1:1– 2:2; Ps 30; Is 12:2–6; Mt 28:1–10

'Cry out for joy and gladness.'

(Isaiah 12:6a)

The day begins on a sombre note. Holy Saturday, for all its potential anticipation, still rightly lingers in the solemnity of Good Friday. The tomb has been closed, the pathos and drama of the preceding days buried in the damp, freshly turned earth. Only the women, clutching their grief in the ointments and oils with which they busy themselves, frequent the barren place. We too, if we are honest with ourselves, find ourselves in a familiar place, the place where we live most of our lives. A dull, aching place in which we avoid too much pain and, consequently too much joy, by burrowing into our routines, clutching our cheque–books and diaries against the possible unwanted surprises of a day. And yet, how it will end, this day!

The grey slush of late winter still lingers on the streets. For weeks now, our newspaper features have shown no colour but the gunmetal grey of tanks and military hardware and the dry brown of scorched and devastated desert landscapes. This painful war in Iraq holds us in its terrible thrall. It is the weary mid–point of our lives. I am in the living room, listening to my husband's measured voice as it floats out of the radio. He, a teacher of social ethics, has been asked to carefully explain the intricacies of the just war tradition for a local radio talk show. When we were younger, it seemed as though the world could be made new – whether through our own limitless energy, our peace corps, our affirmative actions, the dawning of the Age of Aquarius, or whatever. We were going to make love, not war. That seems a very long time ago.

I turn from the radio to a video series I am requiring my students to view: 'A Force More Powerful: Non–Violent Movements of the Twentieth Century'. Gandhi wresting India's independence from the British; the Solidarity Movement in Poland advocating union organizing and creating the conditions for the demise of Communist rule; the sit–ins at lunch counters that desegregated the city of Nashville early in the civil rights movement; the non–violent tactics of economic boycotts that helped bring down the apartheid system in South Africa. I am energized by the bracing possibilities, consoled by the imaginative capacity of human beings to bring something so radical, so new, to birth. Maybe it is possible that the stone was, and still can be, rolled away.

Thought of the day

'Let us not tire of preaching love; it is the force that will overcome the world. Though we see that waves of violence succeed in drowning the fire of Christian love, love must win out. It is the only thing that can. We have never preached violence, except the violence of love, which left Christ nailed to a cross . . .' (Oscar Romero)

Prayer

God who is beyond imagining,
stretch our imaginations to something of your size.
God whose gentle power dislodged the most immovable of stones,
Clear away all that obstructs us from living your shalom.
Amen.

Dancing in the morning

Acts 10:34, 37–43; Ps 118; Col 3:1–4; Jn 20:1–9

> *'When Christ is revealed – and he is your life – you too will be revealed in all your glory.'*
>
> (Colossians 3:4)

Years ago, at a parish noted for its experimental liturgy, I witnessed the resurrection in a dance. The performer was a young man, tall and lithe, muscular with the sinewy strength of the well–trained dance artist. He had, I knew, recently returned from a trial period spent in a religious community. And for some time he had been struggling with his deep religious sensibilities and with questions about his sexual orientation, wondering what God wanted of him and how he was to best live faithfully.

His dance was not originally planned as part of the liturgical celebration. After the reading of the gospel text, the choir was to sing what is my favourite Easter hymn. With its poetic text it captures both a sense of nature's springtime transmutation and the radical transformation of reality presaged in the resurrection. It reminds us that Easter is just that: created matter, in all its unique particular beauty, glorified from within.

> Now the green blade rises
> From the buried grain,
> Wheat that in dark earth
> Many days has lain;
> Love lives again,
> That with the dead has been;

Love is come again
Like wheat arising green.

A day or so in advance, the young dancer showed up and it was agreed that he should dance the Green Blade song. None of us saw him perform until the service itself. As the music began, our attention was directed toward a white cloth lying on the floor just before the altar. Beneath it, the subtlest of movement could be seen. Gradually the cloth slipped aside and he lay there, dressed only in a white loincloth, his long dancer's limbs stretched out in a corpse–like pose. From deep within, the subtlest energy grew. With head and feet still touching the floor, his central body inched up until it rose by itself off the ground. Then slowly, ever so slowly, with what did not seem like ordinary human movement, he rose. Every muscle engaged without seeming effort, he arrived at full stature then, palms up, arms raised slightly to each side; he began to move out of the sanctuary toward the congregation. He grazed the altar steps, moving out into the central aisle, down which he travelled with infinite grace, each slow patient step propelled by some incomprehensible inner yearning that allowed him to barely touch the carpeted floor. As he exited out the front doors of the church, the song ended. We were enveloped in a thick silence.

Raised from the dead,
My risen Lord is seen;
Love is come again
Like wheat arising green.

Thought for the day

'All of a sudden I perceived that the silence was a

presence. At the heart of the silence was he who is all stillness, all peace, all poise.' (George Bernanos)

Prayer

When our hearts are wintry,
Grieving, or in pain,
Your touch can call us back to life again,
Fields of our hearts that dead and bare have been;
Love is come again
Like wheat arising green.

Notes

Sources for the Thoughts for the day quotes used by Wendy Wright in her Holy Week reflections:

Sunday: Thomas Merton, '"Blessed Are the Meek": The Christian Roots of Non–Violence', in *The Non–Violent Alternative*, ed. Gordon Zahn, New York: Farrar, Strauss and Giroux, 1980, p. 212.

Monday: Charles Peguy. Quoted in *The Dorothy Day Book*, ed. Margaret Quigley and Michael Garvey, Springfield, IL: Templeton, 1982, p. 92.

Tuesday: Oscar Romero. Quoted in *Romero: A Life* by James Brockman, Maryknoll: Orbis Books 1989, pp. 230–31.

Wednesday: Martin Luther King, Jr. *Strength to Love*. Philadelphia: Fortress Press, 1987, p. 38.

Thursday: Martin Buber. Quoted in *The Dorothy Day Book*, p. 27.

Friday: Dorothy Day. Quoted in *Words of Peace: Selections from the Writings of Dorothy Day*, ed. Mary Evelyn Jegen. Pax Christi USA, 1989, p. 22.

Saturday: Oscar Romero. Quoted in Brockman, *Romero*, p. 18.

Sunday: George Bernanos. Quoted in *The Dorothy Day Book*, p. 100.

'Now the Green Blade Rises' (Text: John M.C. Crum © Oxford University Press).

About CAFOD

CAFOD is a major British charity that has been fighting third world poverty since 1962. We believe that all human beings have a right to dignity and respect and that the world's resources are a gift to be shared by all men and women, whatever their race, nationality or religion.

CAFOD is the English and Welsh arm of Caritas Internationalis, a worldwide network of Catholic relief and development organisations. With the help of our network of regional organisers throughout England and Wales, CAFOD works in partnership on over 1000 programmes worldwide.

We raise money in England and Wales to finance:

- **Long-term development work:**
  Work with some of the world's poorest communities. Programmes include education and skills training, health care, safe water, and agricultural and small business development.
- **Emergencies:**
  Immediate help for people affected by emergencies such as wars and natural disasters.
- **Analysis** of the causes of underdevelopment.
- **Campaigns** on behalf of the world's poor.
- **Education** in England and Wales that raises awareness of the causes of third world poverty and promotes change.

Website: Cafod.org.uk